poems that fit in a shoe

Alex Gildzen

Luchador Press

Big Tuna, Texas

Copyright © Alex Gildzen, 2024

First edition 1 3 5 7 9 10 8 6 4 2

ISBN: 978-1-958182-75-8

LCCN: 2024940020

Author photo: Anthony-Masterson

Cover image: Alex Gildzen, "Shoe-Na-Ku," 2024

Acknowledgments:

The author thanks the many editors and publishers who have presented his poems over these decades.

TABLE OF CONTENTS

1. Collectd Short Poems

Nearkus - from My First Trip to Europe

28 sept 1973: London / 67

29 sept: London / 67

30 sept: London / 68

1 oct: London / 68

2 oct: London / 68

3 oct: London / 69

4 oct: London / 69

5 oct: London / 69

6 oct: London / 70

7 oct: London / 70

8 oct: London/Dover / 70

9 oct: Calais/Paris / 71

10 oct: Paris / 71

11 oct: Paris / 73

12 oct: Zurich/Milan / 74

13 oct: Bologna / 74

14 oct: Bologna / 75

15 oct: Bologna/Florence / 75

16 oct: Florence/Arezzo / 77

17 oct: Florence / 77

18 oct: Florence / 77

19 oct: Florence/Santa Giuliana / 78

20 oct: Santa Giuliana/Perugia/Rome / 78

21 oct: Rome / 78

22 oct: Rome / 79

23 oct: Rome/NYC / 79

1 oct 2022: Palm Springs / 79

poems that fit in a shoe

1.

COLLECTD SHORT POEMS

(1962-2023)

Waves tap the side of the boat.

I head it to that distant spot

where clouds meet water

leaving behind mistakes.

Go back, go back, go back says the water.

I smile and speed ahead.

1962

ON MIRO'S "THE POETESS"

I see a man,
    a bird,
    a star,
    a fish —
yet all
becomes a whole,
      a poem,
      a glorious constellation.

1962

I pause
near the end of

my coffeebreak
to contemplate

Amadeo Modigliani's
eyesight: how sublime

to see swans
with human heads.

1964

Oh, bitter cold it was
like Keats had never known,

and my fingers had lost
their feel for feeling.

I had been to the edge
of the sea and the edge

was cold and the sea
was wet and I came home

too numb to know
you were wearing a black dress.

1965

VARIATION ON BRIDGES

I've loved flowers that fade
soon after blooming

and songs forgotten
before their notes are done.

So I speak this poem
and let it die.

1965

You roam through fields of me,
catching ladybugs in cupped hands,
then hide in circles of sun
leaving me no map to follow.

Soon the moon moves through trees
and points to a slow river flow.
I stop to bathe my burns
and find you waiting in the water.

1965

FOR SUSAN LINCOLN

paper dolls, a panda bear and me
stuffed upon your crowded shelf

tomorrow we remember
where we left the mittens and the muff

1965

FOOTNOTE

Maud gun-
ned down
a poet
to become
John's bride
but after
John died
it was
Willie's poems
that kept
Maud alive.

1966

WORDS WHISPERED BETWEEN
GREEN SHEETS

die there.

My later pen cannot revive
them.

Instead I place rosebuds on
this bed

and pray for our dead
words.

1967

IN THE SILENCE, IN THE SPRING

Starting again,
not sure if May might bring snow,
I cuddle in the corner of your eye
hiding from the wind.

1967

Times words won't come
come often now,
not like fawn days
dazed by dry twigs.

1967

LAST WORDS FOR MY SONS

I autograph the wind,

will it to you, ask only

that you ride the curl

of crossed t's, toss,

splash down hard. And,

yes, don't look long at stars;

they burn holes in your eyes.

1967

ON WINNING A PRIZE

for Gwendolyn Brooks

Words torn from flesh

fall heavy on those

who know tearing;

we have toiled

in these red fields

and still sing.

1967

FOR D.A. LEVY

to establish tranquility
in a sunburst
                    he leaves
cleave-land for
auckland island
or zambia
wherever his stamps
take him

1968

Worms mulch in such bafflement.
Ants make mounds of it.

My wave length extends
only to a few.

The rest of the time I'm enclaved
in this silly cave of words.

1968

PREFACE TO "THE MADAGASCAR POEMS"

for Kenneth Koch

That silly blonde line

curved romantically

around her antimacassar

& I knew,

without even guessing,

what wit

her sandwiches wd hold.

                    1968

AUGUST

Malaise of wasted days
and boring moonless nights
changes people into bugs
and slow pregnant creatures.

I have become a slug
crawling through my spittle.

1968

BURSTING FORTH FROM WINTER

bone snow over cat grave:

                    spare decemberscape

but dance of dandling flakes

                    stirs wind to flame

1969

LINES ON A SAD AFTERNOON

Let's kill the car.
Let's just slip through the night
and crush its skull before it crushes ours

and then we can walk
in clean January air
across frozen lake
and into town.

1969

OCCASIONAL POEM

I wonder what they really thought
hop-scotching across the gray,

but perhaps it's better
not to know of apple dumplings
or Hasselblad headaches
or concealed souvenirs.

O, if only we could have sent
Marianne Moore to the moon.

1969

FOR JAMES BERTOLINO

Trying to make sticks root,
I change water weekly and
wait for signs of growth.

Sometimes there's a green
scum on the water and
some sticks easter.
Soon others rot.

1969

PAPER CUT

quick blood

edge of page
cut deeper
than its poem

1976

CORN POEM

come city poet
calm pill pace
pack chic past

come pick corn

                    1977

from POSTCARD POEMS

memory jogtrots thru the blood
till a pinch of ginger jangles
then the corridors of the past
spill into a ballroom of pocked parquet

1977

THE NEED TO RETURN TO

rocking in my dream gondola
I start to stare again
at the gold of yr star
marvel at the worshippers
you gain with each new stunt:

      whipping a horse with gladioli
      reaching the hunt by warship
      tripping a gladiator in a store
      riding the rim off a hearse

          1977

LAND WHOSE LANGUAGE IS A FIST

every minute of morning
tightens noose around neck
each spoon of afternoon
brims over with gall

but come night
tip of Oahu's highest wave
won't be pillow enough
for the moon we'll make

1978

POEM BEGINNING WITH A LINE FROM
A LETTER TO STANLEY KRIPPNER

the trees edging the lake are a tartan shawl.
you can wear it or not on a fall night..
but don't shake its old folds
or there won't be warmth to wrap
your shoulders in.

1978

READING HAFIZ IN BILLIE DOVE'S BEDROOM
ON A RAINY MORNING

falling pattern
                    regular as shawl tatting
covering one window

thru rose petals
                    woven in brown & gold threads

past wet palms
                    a glimpse of red tile roof
dull before gray of a sky
I wanted to welcome me with sun

1979

BILLET-DOUX IN THE MORNING

for Robert Drivas

snow quilt outside the window

no quilt on us

                        so I wake shivering

to watch you buried beneath a pillow

I kiss your nipples till you smile

it's time for tea

                        for me to go home

1979

DIVORCE OF SLEEP

our entwined bodies   continents apart:

he travels without passport
twitching like a cat

while I chase words
wait for him to wake

to write our poem of morning

1979

A SILKWORM LISTENS TO BIZET

shedding my skin again

between mulberry feasts

I require warmth & sweet air

when the music is this good

my head in twists of eight

spins finer white silk

1979

FOR JOHN LENNON

a gun   again

                        1980

JANIS AT MONTEREY

13 years later

we still echo
a dead mama's wow

& heat our ink
on your fire

1980

FALL FLOW

for r.j.s.

bees keep time within
releasing it for us
to sweeten our tea with

1980

GOOD-BY GLORIA

you'd look at the trees out there

dressed by Edith Head

in this season's colors

give us the big pout & say

"pretty way to die"

1981

MONK MARKS

scars & burns
Thelonius left
on Lennon's white piano
I'd exhibit
like Whitman's marginalia
or Turner's palette
reminders that art is made

1982

FOR TENNESSEE WILLIAMS

when the prince of pain
choked on the night
no Christopher Flanders
drew off his rings

the only angel there
made his words wings
to lift sorrow
into flight

1983

WALKING TO NAUTILUS
ON A SEPTEMBER MORNING
BEFORE SUNRISE

deathbed kiss of the moon

ice shot to the sphincter

1984

TAKAEZU :

        3 SPOUTED POEM

        in the yard

counting peonies

        at the dump

gathering ash

        among cabbages

smelling roses

        1986

TANKA ARGENTINO

in Buenos Aires
on a steamy afternoon
we liberate clothes
you take me into yr mouth
& the skies open with rain

1988

BARCELONA LUNA

on the tiny stage

       of La Bodega Bohemia

           off the Ramblas

an old queen

       flashd castanets

          & made us a moon

because there was none in the sky

          1989

NOVEMBER ROSES

remember that morning
before rain turnd to snow

when I pickd
roses for you

you kissd the wet petals
I tastd the rain on yr lips

I taste that rain
every day you're gone

1989

BREAKFAST AT A RESTAURANT WITH
NO NAME IN INDEPENDENCE VA

silver-toothd man
in Stetson & shitkickers
calld us "sweet boys"
as he stubbd out
his cigaret in his eggs

1991

szechuan roses

stuck in pot

or hot on plate

another edible garden

1993

SUMMER'S END

in memory of Paul Monette

it's all blurr & whirr

beating of wings

& buzz of throat

that dash from fading flower

to feeder

in search of the sweet

that persistence to live

is a jolt of joy

1997

NIJINSKY'S UNDERWEAR

threads that held him
slide across my lips
burning me with the fire
in his leap

sniffing the ash
keeps the dance alive

1999

RAILROAD ROSARY

I see Carl Sandburg's face
every time I train thru Galesburg

like the Elkhart flowerheart
or El Rancho Hotel in Gallup

I tell these beads to know
how far I am from home

1999

MARMONT MOON

it's full

over the pool

a cat

stalks undergrowth

while I pine

in the dark

for the boy

on the billboard

2000

there are men
we meet in the nite
who shine like gems
then are gone forever

as I grow gray
memory makes
a bracelet of them
which I wear to bed
so that their shining
brings dreams

2002

the poet
lights the candle
that isn't there

2015

WIRES FROM
THE SCREEN DOOR

Buddy Guy
used them
to make
his first guitar

no keeping
the music inside
from getting out

2015

MORNING MOON

last kiss

of

nite already dead

2016

SOMETIMES I VISIT CHARLIE FARRELL

I ask him
how it was
back then
in Palm Springs

he never answers
but the breeze
thru the grass
around his tombstone
whispers secrets

2017

MORNING AFTER
MY 75th BIRTHDAY

the mountains

are still there

& will be

after I'm dead

& this poem

disappears

2018

CEYLON CINNAMON
ON GOLDEN DELICIOUS

for Michelle Fiore

sometimes

simple joys

are best

2020

FOR ROBERT HANSEN

fill a thimble
or city watertank

art
has no boundaries

drip or deluge
can change lives

2021

the morning
I wrote
2 poems
before coffee
I felt
like John Dorsey

2022

donut peach
peach donut

different but
both delicious

2022

MADONNA INN

rock wall
rainbow ceiling

no need to sleep

my room
is a waking dream

2023

MY WARHOLS

Marilyn & Alice B. Shoe
gone for decades
bring tears
where smiles
were when
I bought them

2023

PUTTING TOGETHER
THIS BOOK

2 lines

a corsage

4 lines

a hammer

2023

2.

**Nearkus
from My First Trip to Europe**

(poems woven from threads in a travel diary)

> for Jeff Wietor
> who droppd the seed
> that became this plant

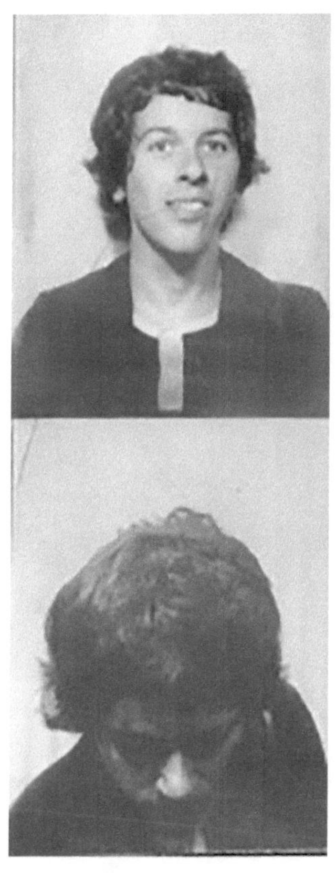

(photo taken in a photo booth in Dover before crossing the
Channel on the Chantilly)

28 sept 1973: London

arr'd
after no sleep

walkd
from air terminal
to Eden House

took tube
got off prematurely
walkd more

29 sept: London

got lost

new shoes

sore feet

30 sept: London

sitting in Berkeley Square
listening for nightingales
that aren't there
& thinking of Leslie Howard

1 oct: London

after breakfast
left David's

met Roberta
at Biba

2 oct: London

morning
sunny & cool

evening
pub-crawling

3 oct: London

after Alec Guinness
rhinewine at Markham's Pub
listening to David Bowie

4 oct: London

steak pudding at Pimlico Tram
white wine at County Alms
tea with Bessie Love
salad at Mowat's
drinks at Tom Cribb's

5 oct: London

"dull & misty start" (BBC)
before
"Floating World" (Victoria & Albert)
then
"The Farm" (Royal Court)

6 oct: London

the foreign girl
wakes me
for breakfast

7 oct: London

with Lem Kitaj
a Don Siegel film

then
Sandra Fisher's spaghetti
with R. B.

8 oct: London/Dover

last pint of bitter in England
at The Albion
homey local
run by
loquacious Hilda
& quiet Bob

9 oct: Calais/Paris

bad day
in Calais

10 oct: Paris

my Hockney day
(& nite)

running into him
on Saint-Germain-des-Pres

at Cafe de Flore
we join Shirley Goldfarb

drawing me 3 times
at Cour de Rohan

dinner together
at La Coupole

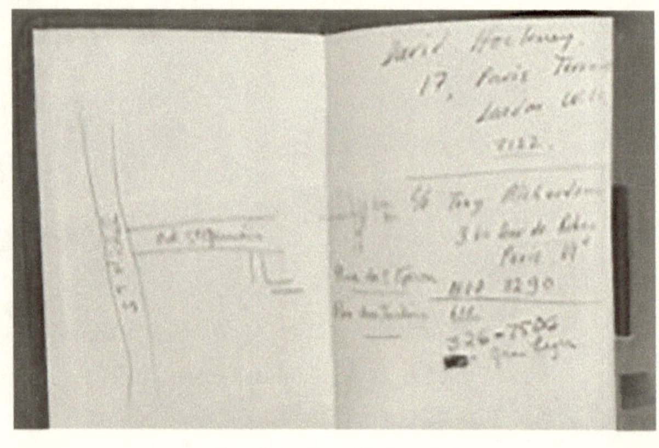

(map drawn by Hockney in front pastedown of travel diary)

11 oct: Paris

walk from Gare de l'Est
to Pere Lachaise

metro to Notre Dame

walk to Shakespeare & Co

Chaplin film
with French subtitles

drinks at David's
before dinner together
at Restaurant des Beaux Arts

12 oct: Zurich/Milan

train thru rain
from France
to Switzerland

a museum
& hot chocolate

more train
to Italy

13 oct: Bologna

with my hosts
Mary Jane & W. S. DiPiero
in a church yard
seeing a French film

14 oct: Bologna

climbing towers
risotto & writing

my hosts & I
join Rosa & Marino Bosinelli
for drinks

15 oct: Bologna/Florence

another city
another host

Sheila Tabakoff

we dine
on beefsteak Florentine
with fennel
at La Beppa

16 oct: Florence/Arezzo

joins Sheila's students
to see frescoes
of Piero della Francesca

17 oct: Florence

the Davids

Michelangelo's
&
Donatello's

18 oct: Florence

first Italian meal
orderd alone

then drinks
at Harry's Bar

meal cheaper
than the drinks

19 oct: Florence/Santa Giuliana
reading Ashbery
by the fire
in this house
sans electricity

20 oct: Santa Giuliana/Perugia/Rome

morning of writing
on old wall
near base
of tallest tower
of Sheila's castle

21 oct: Rome

Rome
does not exist
in daylight

it only lives
at nite

22 oct: Rome

Herald Tribune
reports preparations
for Nixon's impeachment

23 oct: Rome/NYC

at DaVinci
strike of airport staff

even Italian president
can't take off

all the hours on the ground
make me miss my connection at JFK

---

1 oct 2022: Palm Springs

what I left out then
cd be a novel now

& a note for the curious

"Italian Sketches" — a quartet of prose poems written on
this trip — were collectd in The Avalanche of Time (1985).

Poems by **Alex Gildzen** have appeared in a coloring book, a dozen anthologies, at least a hundred magazines and a bench in downtown Palm Springs. A multiple Pushcart Prize nominee, he has won the President's Medal at Kent State University and an Ohioana Award. He has edited *Dress: Journal of the Costume Society of America* and co-edited *A Gathering of Poets*. Gildzen's photographs have appeared in *Plain Dealer Sunday Magazine* and *New York Times Style Magazine* as well as book covers for NiteBallet Press, Crisis Chronicles Press and Poems-for-All. He was featured in the documentary "Big Joy" and has been an extra in mainstream films and a supporting player in independent films. He has been a model, with and without clothes, for painters and photographers.

This project was made possible, in part, by generous support from the Osage Arts Community.

Osage Arts Community provides temporary time, space and support for the creation of new artistic works in a retreat format, serving creative people of all kinds — visual artists, composers, poets, fiction and nonfiction writers. Located on a 152-acre farm in an isolated rural mountainside setting in Central Missouri and bordered by ¾ of a mile of the Gasconade River, OAC provides residencies to those working alone, as well as welcoming collaborative teams, offering living space and workspace in a country environment to emerging and mid-career artists. For more information, visit us at www.osageac.org